EXPECT THE WORsT

EXPECT THE WORST

(YOU WON'T BE DISAPPOINTED)

Pessimistic Thoughts on Life, People, Relationships, Family,
Work, Politics, and the State of the World

ERIC MARCUS

HarperSanFrancisco
A Division of HarperCollins*Publishers*

All quotes by Ashleigh Brilliant copyright © 1992.
Quote by Kathy Holder copyright © 1989 by OZ, a Division of Andrews and McMeel.
Copyright acknowledgments continue on page 127.

Text Design by Irene Imfeld

FIRST EDITION

Library of Congress Cataloging-in-Publication Data
Marcus, Eric.
   Expect the worst (you won't be disappointed) : pessimistic
thoughts on life, people, relationships, family, work, politics,
and the state of the world / Eric Marcus. — 1st ed.
      p.   cm.
   ISBN 0-06-250997-7 (alk. paper)
   1. Pessimism—Quotations, maxims, etc.   2. Aphorisms
and apothegms.   3. Quotations, English.   I. Title.
BJ1477.M287   1992
149'.6—dc20   91-59032
                                                          CIP

92 93 94 95 96 ❖ BANTA 10 9 8 7 6 5 4 3 2

To my Grandma Ethel, who always told me,
"I'll never live to see you married."
(She was right.)

CONTENTS

ACKNOWLEDGMENTS

In a world filled with hopeless optimists, I was heartened to discover more than a handful of kindred spirits who have never doubted that the glass is indeed half empty.

To those who contributed their original bleak thoughts to Expect the Worst, I am probably forever grateful (with "forever," you can never be too sure). You'll find your names throughout the book attached to your contributions. And many thanks to those of you who brought appropriately pessimistic quotes to my attention, particularly Robert Abramson, Simeon Baum, Lila Bellar, Frank Browning, Tina Collen, Leonore Fleischer, David Frankel, Robert Getlan, Joan Lexau, Ann Northrop, Barry Owen, Donald Poynter, Joel Roselin, Toni Sciarra, Randy Shilts, Christian Skeem, Georgette Weir, and John Wolf.

For inspiration, at those times when I felt vaguely optimistic, I depended on a small group of world-class naysayers, including Posy Gering, Cynthia Grossman, and Hunter Madsen.

And finally, I want to acknowledge my editor, Barbara Moulton, a hopeless optimist who has never had any doubts about the potential success of Expect the Worst. *I'm sure she'll be disappointed.*

INTRODUCTION

Against my better judgment I let my editor convince me to do this book. From the very first time we talked I was certain the project was doomed. "Who would buy it?" I asked. "I know I could never do it," I protested. "I'll never meet the deadline," I warned.

But the more emphatic I became, the more my editor became convinced that I was the perfect person to put together a book of pessimistic quotes. I had the right attitude, she thought, and even better, I had the right genetic inspiration. She already knew about my Grandma Ethel, one of the all-time great pessimists.

Grandma Ethel, who I must point out was a very good-hearted and devoted grandmother, was not the most positive person in the world. For example, after the first hard freeze each winter she called to remind me not to walk on frozen ponds because I might fall through the ice and drown. These calls were inevitably followed by newspaper clippings about children who had paid the ultimate price for walking on thin ice. I always took these warnings very seriously, even though the nearest body of water was the Atlantic Ocean—more than ten miles away. To this day, I have never walked on a frozen pond, although I'm sure it will happen one aberrant happy-go-lucky day when I'm not paying attention to where I'm going.

With Grandma as my inspiration, and with the help of many fellow "nabobs of negativism," nattering or otherwise (to borrow from Spiro Agnew), I have created Expect the Worst (You Won't Be Disappointed). *I like to think of it as something of an antidote to the endless saccharine tide of books with titles like,* Living Happily Ever After, The Joy of Visualization, *or* Living in the Light. *Can we possibly stand one more book that tells us how to achieve inner peace—or excellent health—by thinking kind thoughts?*

So if you're looking for just a few reminders—and heaven forbid, a few laughs—about the way things really are, you've come to the right place. Then again, what I find funny and what you find funny are probably two entirely different things, but I promised my editor I would do Expect the Worst, *and a promise is a promise. At least I don't feel guilty, because I've warned her from the very beginning that* Expect the Worst *will probably be an incredible flop. Unfortunately she thinks I'm just being funny.*

Just a note about the attributions. Where no birth/death dates are given, that means the quoted individual is alive (I hope), or I simply could not locate birth/death information.

To those I've misquoted and/or to whom I've failed to give appropriate credit, my apologies. If you contact me at the address below, I'll make corrections in a later printing (Another printing?

Who am I kidding?). And, finally, if you've got a great pessimistic thought that you'd like to share, write to me at Harper San Francisco, 1160 Battery Street, San Francisco, CA 94111.

If I'm lucky, maybe someone at Harper San Francisco will remember who I am and forward your letter, assuming I haven't fallen through the ice

Eric Marcus
May, 1992

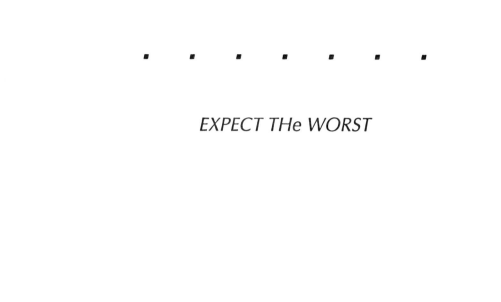

EXPECT THe WORST

LIFE

When it came to her view of life, I always thought of my Grandma Ethel as a world-class pessimist. But that was before Leonore Fleischer wrote to me about her mother, Helen, whom Leonore suggested could fill Expect the Worst—and a few sequels besides—with her pessimistic thoughts. Leonore wrote: "If you will send me a self-addressed, mother-size box, with a couple of air holes and the proper postage, I will ship you my own personal mother, a woman who, when faced with the classic dilemma 'Is the glass half full or half empty?' can, at one and the same time and without apparent effort, convince you that (a) there is no glass—you're running a temperature and hallucinating; and (b) *the glass is chipped and dirty and if you drink from it you'll catch a fatal disease." Sorry Grandma. In the realm of pessimism, Leonore's mom sets a standard that even you can't meet.*

*B*irth, *n. The first and direst of all disasters.*

—*Ambrose Bierce (1842–1914?)*

*W*e're all in this alone.

—*Lily Tomlin*

Our birth is nothing but our death begun.

—Edward Young (1683–1765)

It is a misery to be born, a pain to live, a trouble to die.

—St. Bernard of Clairvaux (1090–1153)

I've learned to accept birth and death but sometimes I still worry about what lies between.

—Ashleigh Brilliant

I can remember, at the age of five, being told that childhood was the happiest period of life (a blank lie, in those days). I wept inconsolably, wished I were dead, and wondered how I should endure the boredom of the years to come.

—Bertrand Russell (1872–1970)

My mother often told me, "Marshall, the sooner you learn that life is 95 percent misery and only 5 percent happiness, the better off you'll be."

—Marshall Kirk

Life is easier than you'd think; all that is necessary is to accept the impossible, do without the indispensable, and bear the intolerable.

—Kathleen Norris (1880–1966)

*W*hy torture yourself when life will do it for you?

—Laura Walker

*D*on't worry about tomorrow; who knows what will befall you today?

—Yiddish folk saying

It's fear of failure that keeps me going. It's fear of success that stops me in my tracks.

—Eric Marcus

Take courage! Whatever you decide to do, it will probably be the wrong thing.

—Ashleigh Brilliant

No good deed goes unpunished.

—Clare Boothe Luce (1903–1987)

Never face facts; if you do you'll never get up in the morning.

—Marlo Thomas

Every morning signals a new day during which something can go wrong.

—Bob Uyeda

"What Can You Expect from a Day that Begins with Getting Up?"

—Wendy R. Ellner (entry in a New York magazine competition for original country song titles)

*T*here's no limit to how complicated things can get, on account of one thing always leading to another.

—*E. B. White (1899–1985)*

*I*f it's not one thing, it's two.

—*James B. Ledford (1924–1981)*

*W*hen sorrows come, they come not
    single spies,
But in battalions.

—*King*, Hamlet, *William Shakespeare (1564–1616)*

*L*ife is divided into the horrible and the miserable.

—*Woody Allen*

I'd give up now, but I don't have the time.

—*Jane Belenky*

*N*inety percent of life is miserable—if you're lucky.

—*Eric Marcus*

*L*ife isn't one damn thing after another. It's the same damn thing again and again.

—*Edna St. Vincent Millay (1892–1950)*

*A*n optimist is a guy who has never had much experience.

—*Don Marquis (1878–1937)*

*H*e who expects much can expect little.

—Gabriel García Márquez

*B*lessed is he who expects nothing, for he shall never be disappointed.

—Alexander Pope (1688–1744)

*N*o matter what you order at a restaurant, what everyone else orders will look better.

—*Paulina Borsook*

*T*here are two tragedies in life. One is not to get your heart's desire. The other is to get it.

—*George Bernard Shaw (1856–1950)*

*L*ife is snack or famine.

—*Susan Wolbarst*

*L*ess is less.

—*Variously attributed*

*I*f anything can go wrong, it will.

—Murphy's Law *(said to have been invented by George Nichols in 1949)*

*M*urphy was an optimist.

—*Variously attributed*

I believe in the total depravity of inanimate things . . . the elusiveness of soap, the knottiness of strings, the transitory nature of buttons, the inclination of suspenders to twist and of hooks to forsake their lawful eyes and cleave only unto the hairs of their hapless owner's head.

—Katharine Ashley (1840–1916)

The bread never falls but on its buttered side.

—English proverb

*T*hings are going to get a lot worse before they get worse.
—Lily Tomlin

*E*very day is horrible, so it couldn't get any worse.
—Barbara Giese

*O*ne day I sat thinking almost in despair; a hand fell on my shoulder and a voice said reassuringly: "Cheer up, things could get worse." So I cheered up and, sure enough, things got worse.
—James Hagerty (1901–1981)

*I*t is wisdom in prosperity, when all is as thou wouldst have it, to fear and suspect the worst.

—Desiderius Erasmus (1466–1536)

*T*he light at the end of the tunnel is only a train, and it's not yours anyhow.

—Author unknown

*P*erhaps one day this too will be pleasant to remember.

—Virgil (70–19 B.C.)

I always read the last page of a book first so that if I die before I finish I'll know how it turned out.

—Nora Ephron

*T*he statistics on death are unchanged.

—Author unknown

*T*he situation is hopeless, but not serious.

—*Austrian proverb as remembered by Rick Stryker's grandmother*

*I*t's always darkest before it goes pitch black.

—*Connie Winkler*

*W*hat is the use of straining after an amiable view of things, when a cynical view is most likely to be the true one.
—George Bernard Shaw (1856–1950)

*N*o matter how cynical you get, it is impossible to keep up.
—Lily Tomlin

*B*elieve nothing and be on your guard against everything.
—Latin proverb

It gets harder the more you know. Because the more you find out the uglier everything seems.

—Frank Zappa

To know all is not to forgive all. It is to despise everybody.

—Quentin Crisp

As surely as you try to impress someone, you'll do something stupid.

—*Tamara Valjean*

No matter how you wiggle and dance, the last three drops will go down your pants.

—*Author unknown*

*L*ife is something that happens to you while you're making other plans.

—*Margaret Millar*

*T*he examined life is not worth living.

—*Gloria Steinem as told to Suzanne Braun Levine*

*O*ne hundred thousand lemmings can't be wrong.

—*Graffiti*

*J*ust because you're paranoid doesn't mean they aren't out to get you.

—*Variously attributed*

*D*on't look back. Something might be gaining on you.

—*Satchel Paige (1906–1982)*

*F*or life in general, there is but one decree: Youth is a blunder, manhood a struggle, old age a regret.

—*Benjamin Disraeli (1804–1881)*

*A*fter a year in therapy, my psychiatrist said to me, "Maybe life isn't for everyone."

—*Larry Brown*

*L*ife is just a bowl of pits.

—*Rodney Dangerfield*

*C*heer up, the worst is yet to come.

—*Philander Johnson*

*S*he not only expects the worst, she makes the worst of it when it happens.

—*Michael Arlen (1895–1956)*

*T*his, too, shall pass—just like a kidney stone.

—*Hunter Madsen*

I've always expected the worst, and it's always worse than I expected.

—Henry James (1843–1916)

*N*o issue is so small that it can't be blown out of proportion.

—Stuart Hughes

*D*on't borrow trouble; it will find you soon enough.

—Betsy Rapoport's Mother and "Gram"

*L*ife can be so tragic: You're here today and here tomorrow.

—*Ashleigh Brilliant*

*L*iving is a sickness from which sleep provides relief every sixteen hours. It's a palliative. The remedy is death.

—*Nicolas-Sébastien Chamfort (1741–1794)*

*W*e die before we have learned to live.

—*Stephen Winsten*

*L*ife's a rough business, and nobody will get through it alive.

—Herbert Frankel

*W*e are all dying people.

—Barry Owen

*T*here is no such thing as inner peace. There is only nervous-ness and death.

—Fran Lebowitz

*D*eath is not the end. There remains the litigation over the estate.

—Ambrose Bierce (1842–1914?)

*I*t's always something.

— *Gilda Radner (1947–1989)*

*W*hen my ship comes in, with my luck I'll be at the airport.

— *John Adey*

*E*xpect the worst. (You won't be disappointed.)

— *Eric Marcus*

PEOPLE

Generally speaking, it wasn't in Grandma's nature to trust people. She viewed everyone who came into her little gift shop in Brooklyn as a potential customer and a potential thief—and not necessarily in that order. Often, after browsers had left the store, she'd scan the shelves convinced they'd stolen a china Madonna or a crystal kitty. Not surprisingly, given the amoral state of humankind, even Grandma's innate pessimism underestimated the potential for thievery. Once, when she was in the stockroom, a customer made off with her solid brass cash register, a pre-electronic machine as heavy as a bank vault. She took off after the slow-moving criminal and forced him to turn over his prize. That thief was lucky—Grandma merely pressed charges. She had threatened to break his neck.

You can always rely on a society of equals taking it out on the women.

—*Alan Sillitoe*

Real equality is going to come not when a female Einstein is recognized as quickly as a male Einstein, but when a female schlemiel is promoted as quickly as a male schlemiel.

—*Bella Abzug, as quoted by Marlo Thomas*

*M*en are taught to apologize for their weaknesses, women for their strengths.

—Lois Wyse

*T*he only time a woman really succeeds in changing a man is when he's a baby.

—Natalie Wood (1938–1981)

*M*en have a much better time of it than women. For one thing, they marry later; for another thing, they die earlier.

—H. L. Mencken (1880–1956)

*W*hen I meet a man I ask myself, "Is this the man I want my children to spend their weekends with?"

—Rita Rudner

. . . beware of men who cry. It's true that men who cry are sensitive to and in touch with feelings, but the only feelings they tend to be sensitive to and in touch with are their own.

—Nora Ephron

*T*he more I see of men, the more I like dogs.

—Madame de Staël (1766–1817)

If you pick up a starving dog and make him prosperous, he will not bite you. This is the principal difference between a dog and a man.

—Mark Twain (1835–1910)

The belief in a supernatural source of evil is not necessary; men alone are quite capable of every wickedness.

—Joseph Conrad (1857–1924)

All I care to know is that a man is a human being—that is enough for me; he can't be much worse.

—Mark Twain (1835–1910)

*B*oys will be boys, and so will a lot of middle-aged men.

—F. McKinney (Kin) Hubbard (1868–1930)

*M*en are like toilets; they're either taken or full of it.

—Author unknown

*W*e learn from experience that men never learn anything from experience.

—George Bernard Shaw (1856–1950)

*T*he 100 percent American is 99 percent an idiot.

—*George Bernard Shaw (1856–1950)*

*N*o one ever went broke underestimating the taste of the American public.

—*H. L. Mencken (1880–1956)*

*T*he public is wonderfully tolerant. It forgives everything except genius.

—*Oscar Wilde (1854–1900)*

The difference between genius and stupidity is that genius has its limits.

—*Author unknown*

*H*uman nature is often the greatest deterrent to making an intelligent decision.

—*Author unknown*

Most people would sooner die than think; in fact, they do so.

—*Bertrand Russell (1872–1970)*

Only two things are infinite, the universe and human stupidity, and I'm not sure about the former.

—*Albert Einstein (1879–1955)*

Only the mediocre are always at their best.

—Jean Giraudoux (1882–1944)

The best lack all conviction, while the worst are full of passionate intensity.

—William Butler Yeats (1865–1939)

No one really listens to anyone else, and if you try it for a while you'll see why.

—Mignon McLaughlin

*T*rust everybody, but cut the cards.

—*Finley Peter Dunne (1867–1936)*

*D*o not trust to the cheering, for those very persons would shout as much if you and I were going to be hanged.

—*Oliver Cromwell (1599–1658)*

*I*t is a sin to believe in the evil of others, but it is seldom a mistake.

—H. L. Mencken (1880–1956)

*I*t's silly to go on pretending that under the skin we are all brothers. The truth is more likely that under the skin we are all cannibals, assassins, traitors, liars, hypocrites, poltroons.

—Henry Miller (1891–1980)

*F*riends may come and go, but enemies accumulate.

—Author unknown

*T*he only normal people are the ones you don't know very well.

—*Joe Ancis*

*P*eople—you can't live with 'em, period.

—*Marshall Kirk*

FAMILY

Above all else, Grandma Ethel valued her family. Not—need I even mention it—that her family made her happy. Every summer for as long as I can remember and for as long as my mother can remember, Grandma Ethel came back from summer vacations in the mountains with her half-dozen sisters to proclaim, "I will never, ever, do that again!" But every year as summer approached, Grandma agreed to spend another vacation with her sisters at the same bungalow colony in the Catskills. For weeks in advance she'd predict in the most pessimistic of tones: "It's gonna be awful! We're gonna fight the whole time!" And year after year, she was right.

They fuck you up, your Mum and Dad.
They may not mean to, but they do.
And give you all the faults they had
And add some extra, just for you.

—Philip Larkin (1922–1985)

If it's not one thing it's your mother.

—Variously attributed

As fathers commonly go, it is seldom a misfortune to be fatherless; and considering the general run of sons, as seldom a misfortune to be childless.

—Lord Chesterfield (1694–1773)

The first half of our lives is ruined by our parents and the second half by our children.

—Clarence Darrow (1857–1938)

There's nothing wrong with teenagers that reasoning with them won't aggravate.

—Author unknown

*H*appiness is having a large, loving, caring, close-knit family in another city.

—*George Burns*

*R*elations are simply a tedious pack of people who haven't got the remotest knowledge of how to live, nor the smallest instinct about when to die.

—*Oscar Wilde (1854–1900)*, The Importance of Being Earnest

*I*t's all relatives.

—*Lynda Cury*

LOVE, RELATIONSHIPS & MARRIAGE

Like lemmings in search of a cliff, we humans are inexorably drawn to the promise of love and marriage. And Grandma was no exception to this generally hopeless quest. (After all, half of all marriages today end in divorce. And more ought to.) But contrary to expectation and experience, Grandma succeeded in love. She found a good man. Unfortunately, he died young. This did nothing to improve Grandma's outlook on life.

*L*ove is a fire. But whether it is going to warm your hearth or burn down your house, you can never tell.

—Joan Crawford (1906–1977)

*E*very little girl knows about love. It is only her capacity to suffer because of it that increases.

—Françoise Sagan

*T*he trouble with loving is that pets don't last long enough and people last too long.

—Author unknown

Love is ideal. Marriage is real. The confusion of the two shall never go unpunished.

—*Johann Wolfgang von Goethe (1749–1832)*

If you want to read about love and marriage you've got to buy two separate books.

—*Alan King*

Love, n. A temporary insanity curable by marriage . . .

—*Ambrose Bierce (1842–1914?)*

*E*very man is thoroughly happy twice in his life: just after he has met his first love, and just after he has left his last one.

—H. L. Mencken (1880–1956)

*T*here are two days when a man is a joy: the day one marries him and the day one buries him.

—Jane Bartlett

The poor wish to be rich, the rich wish to be happy, the single wish to be married, and the married wish to be dead.

—Ann Landers

It seemed to me that the desire to get married—which, I regret to say, I believe is basic and primal in women—is followed almost immediately by an equally basic and primal urge—which is to be single again.

—Nora Ephron

Whether you marry or whether you don't, you'll always regret it.

—Paul Brown

The trouble with some women is that they get all excited about nothing—and then marry him.

—Cher

*W*henever you want to marry someone, go have lunch with his ex-wife.

—Shelley Winters

*P*ersonally, I think if a woman hasn't met the right man by the time she's twenty-four, she may be lucky.

—Deborah Kerr

*K*eep your eyes wide open before marriage, and half shut afterwards.

—*Variously attributed*

*T*he woman cries before the wedding; the man afterward.

—*Polish proverb*

*O*ne was never married, and that's his hell; another is, and that's his plague.

—*Robert Burton (1577–1640)*

*B*ride, *n. A woman with a fine prospect of happiness behind her.*

—Ambrose Bierce (1842–1914?)

*Y*ou enter it living and come out a corpse.

—Shalom Aleichem (1859–1916), on the chuppa, the wedding canopy under which Jewish couples marry

*M*en marry because they are tired, women because they are curious; both are disappointed.

—*Oscar Wilde (1854–1900)*, A Woman of No Importance

A marriage is likely to be called happy if neither party ever expected to get much happiness out of it.

—*Bertrand Russell (1872–1970)*

*M*atrimony—the high sea for which no compass has yet been invented.

—*Heinrich Heine (1797–1856)*

*W*hen a girl marries she exchanges the attentions of many men for the inattention of one.

—Helen Rowland (1875–1950)

*T*he surest way to be alone is to get married.

—Gloria Steinem

Marriage, n. The state or condition of a community consisting of a master, a mistress, and two slaves, making in a!l, two.

—Ambrose Bierce (1842–1914?)

Marriage is the only war in which you sleep with the enemy.

—Author unknown

The most difficult year of marriage is the one you're in.

—Franklin P. Jones

*B*efore marriage, a man will lie awake thinking about something you said; after marriage, he'll fall asleep before you finish saying it.

—Helen Rowland (1875–1950)

*T*here is so little difference between husbands you might as well keep the first.

—Adela Rogers St. Johns (1894–1988)

*T*rust your husband, adore your husband, and get as much as you can in your own name.

—*Advice to Joan Rivers from her mother*

*W*hen a man brings his wife flowers for no reason—there's a reason.

—*Molly McGee (1897–1961)*

*M*arriage is a romance in which the hero dies in the first chapter.

—Author unknown

*I*t begins with a prince kissing an angel. It ends with a bald-headed man looking across the table at a fat woman.

—Author unknown

*M*arriage is a fever in reverse: It starts with heat and ends with cold.

—German proverb

*T*he only solid and lasting peace between a man and his wife is doubtless a separation.

—Lord Chesterfield (1694–1773)

*M*en and women, women and men. It will never work.

—Erica Jong

GOD & RELIGION

I've had my doubts about God and religion since the very beginning of my spiritual education. At the tender age of eight, my parents signed me up for Hebrew school, three afternoons a week. Why, I wondered, were my parents, who had no interest in Judaism and great interest in the teachings of oddly named Indian yogis, consigning me to this fate?

That was just the start of my confusion. In Hebrew school I learned that God was good and I was among His chosen people. I also learned from Rabbi Weinberger that I was lucky to even be alive, because six million Jews perished in the Holocaust. (This was a good God?) I also learned that God would punish me if I ever set foot in a church or said the name of the "so-called" savior of the Christian people. (Henceforth he was to be known as

J.C.) But at the same time, I knew that my Grandma Ethel, who owned a small gift shop in an Irish-Catholic Brooklyn neighborhood, did a brisk business in religious objects like wooden crosses, china Madonnas, and little portraits of J.C. Not only was she not *punished* for trading in idolatry, she was *rewarded* financially for selling to the enemy (although there's no telling what happened when she faced her maker).

So it should have come as no surprise to anyone that, by the time I was ready for my Bar Mitzvah, I was pretty certain that God was a fictional character and that, if there was God, He wasn't a very attentive or good God. But I have to admit that whenever I'm in an airplane, thundering down the runway, I cast all my doubts aside and instinctively say the Shema. That's the prayer Jews are supposed to say if they think they're about to die. Just in case there is a God, I figure it couldn't hurt.

I sometimes think that God in creating man somewhat over-estimated his ability.

—Oscar Wilde (1854–1900)

If there's a supreme being, he's crazy.

—Marlene Dietrich (1901–1992)

I'm Jewish. It's Christmas. Things could be better.

—From an ad for Jews for Jesus

*F*ear prophets . . . and those prepared to die for the truth, for as a rule they make many others die with them, often before them, at times instead of them.

—Umberto Eco

God punishes us by giving us the things we desire.

—*Variously attributed*

If God were suddenly condemned to live the life which he has inflicted upon men, He would kill himself.

—*Alexandre Dumas, fils (1824–1895)*

The more you complain, the longer God lets you live.

—*Lapel button spotted by Carol Day*

God is love, but get it in writing.

—*Gypsy Rose Lee (1914–1970)*

HEALTH

To Grandma Ethel the world was a very hostile place that conspired to break our bones, give us colds, and end life early and abruptly. My poor mother, Grandma's only child, was forbidden to do anything risky, like ride a bicycle, swim, or roller skate. I got off easy. As her grandchild I only got warnings. For example, every time it rained, Grandma would call and tell me, "Don't go out in the rain without your galoshes or you'll catch pneumonia and die." I may have been a budding pessimist, but I wasn't ready to die, so I followed her instructions religiously. That was a couple of decades ago; I haven't worn galoshes since. Still, whenever I go out in the rain, I feel like I'm tempting the gods, *especially because I can hear this little voice with a heavy Polish accent whispering, "People still die from pneumonia. Don't say I didn't warn you."*

*E*arly to rise and early to bed
Makes a male healthy, wealthy, and dead.

—James Thurber (1894–1961)

*D*octors are men who prescribe medicines of which they know little, to cure diseases of which they know less, in human beings of whom they know nothing.

—Voltaire (1694–1778)

The only way to keep your health is to eat what you don't want, drink what you don't like, and do what you'd rather not.

—Mark Twain (1835–1910)

The cardiologist's diet: If it tastes good, spit it out.

—Paulina Borsook

After my dad's heart attack he stopped smoking, cut back on drinking, and avoided eating fun food. When I told him, "Isn't it nice that you'll live longer," he told me in a really disgusted voice, "You don't really live longer. It just seems like it."

—Nina Puglia

A diet is a plan, generally hopeless, for reducing your weight, which tests your willpower but does little for your waistline.

—Herbert B. Prochnow

*L*ong meals make short lives.

—Sir John Lubbock, Lord Avebury (1834–1915)

*I*f it tastes good, it's trying to kill you.

—Roy Qualley

*I*t's no longer a question of staying healthy. It's a question of finding a sickness you like.

—Jackie Mason

*Q*uit worrying about your health. It'll go away.

—Robert Orben

AGING

Grandma never had anything good to say about getting old. And why should she? Her arches fell, her eyesight failed, her gums retreated, and everything ached (so she constantly told us). I was very young at the time and wondered what all the complaining was about. "Getting old can't be that bad," I thought. Well, not long ago, as an orthopedic surgeon manipulated my hip, trying to determine what was causing me agonizing pain every time I took a step, I realized that not only was getting old that bad, with all its aches, pains, wrinkles, and gray hair, but it starts when you're young and goes on for a long time. If you're lucky.

*H*e that is not handsome at twenty, nor strong at thirty, nor rich at forty, nor wise at fifty, will never be handsome, strong, rich, or wise.

—George Herbert (1593–1633)

*A*t thirty man suspects himself a fool;
Knows it at forty, and reforms his plan;
At fifty chides his infamous delay,
Pushes his prudent purpose to resolve;
In all his magnanimity of thought
Resolves; and re-solves; then dies the same.

—Edward Young (1683–1765)

*O*ne starts to get young at the age of sixty, and then it's too late.

—Pablo Picasso (1881–1973)

*Y*ou remember I used to say I wanted to die at thirty—well, I'm now twenty-nine and the prospect is still welcome.

—F. Scott Fitzgerald (1896–1940)

*W*hen you are as old as I, young man, you will know there is only one thing in the world worth living for, and that is sin.

—Lady Speranze Wilde (1821–1896), mother of Oscar Wilde

From birth to age eighteen, a girl needs good parents, from eighteen to thirty-five she needs good looks, from thirty-five to fifty-five she needs a good personality, and from fifty-five on she needs cash.

—Sophie Tucker (1884–1966)

Say the woman is forty-four.
Say she is five-seven-and-a-half.
Say her hair is stick colour.
Say her eyes are chameleon.
Would you put her in a sack and bury her,
suck her down into the dumb dirt?
   Some would,
   If not, time will.

—Anne Sexton (1928–1974)

'Tis strange, that it is not in vogue to commit hara-kari as the Japanese do at sixty. Nature is so insulting in her hints and notices, does not pull you by the sleeve, but pulls out your teeth, tears off your hair in patches, steals your eyesight, twists your face into an ugly mask, in short, puts all contumelies upon you, without in the least abating your zeal to make a good appearance, and all this is at the same time that she is moulding the new figures around you into wonderful beauty which of course is only making your plight worse.

—Ralph Waldo Emerson (1803–1882)

Brain weight peaks at about twenty-five, and the number of critical cells, after a period of constancy from birth to the early twenties, declines sharply to the nineties. Each day of our adult lives more than 100,000 nerve cells die and nerve cells are never, of course, replaced.

—Lord Rothschild (1911–1990)

You should live well into your senility and beyond.

—Heard on "Garrison Keillor's American Radio Company"

POLITICS

When it comes to politics and politicians, I'm a hard-core pessimist. Given the state of politics here and abroad, it's hard not to be. In fact, I have yet to meet anyone who is optimistic about politics, except perhaps a politician. I used to write speeches for an elected official in Queens, New York. He was a happy-go-lucky kind of guy. Everyone liked him. He seemed to love his job. Then one day he was implicated as a central figure in a major New York City bribery scandal, and he stuck a steak knife through his heart. I still haven't been able to shake this uneasy feeling that his decision to end it all had something to do with the last speech I wrote for him, and cutting into a steak has never been the same.

*R*eader, suppose you were an idiot and suppose you were a member of Congress. But I repeat myself.

—Mark Twain (1835–1910)

I don't think that cynicism, disgust, and apathy is anything other than a really intelligent response to the state of American politics.

—Molly Ivins

*T*hose who are too smart to engage in politics are punished by being governed by those who are dumber.

—Plato (ca. 428–348 B.C.)

*P*ublic office is the last refuge of the incompetent.

—Boies Penrose (1860–1921)

*D*emocracy is being allowed to vote for the candidate you dislike least.

—*Robert Byrne*

*V*ote for the man who promises least. He'll be the least disappointing.

—*Bernard M. Baruch (1870–1965)*

*I*t doesn't matter who you vote for, the government always gets in.

—*London graffiti*

*P*olitics, n. The conduct of public affairs for private advantage.

—*Ambrose Bierce (1842–1914?)*

*T*he first mistake in public business is the going into it.

—*Benjamin Franklin (1706–1790)*

*N*o man will carry out of the presidency the reputation which carried him into it.

—*Thomas Jefferson (1743–1826)*

*E*very revolution evaporates and leaves behind the slime of a new bureaucracy.

—*Franz Kafka (1883–1924)*

You are better off not knowing how sausages and laws are made.

—Author unknown

Who thinks the Law has anything to do with Justice? It's what we have because we can't have justice.

—William McIlvanney

*S*enate, *n. A body of elderly gentlemen charged with high duties and misdemeanors.*

—Ambrose Bierce (1842–1914?)

*W*hen I was a boy I was told that anybody could become president; I'm beginning to believe it.

—Clarence Darrow (1857–1938)

*Y*ou want a friend in Washington? Get a dog.

—Harry S. Truman (1884–1972)

THE STATE OF THE WORLD

All her life Grandma Ethel looked on the state of the world with a jaundiced eye. She had good reason. Ethel Sand was born at the end of the nineteenth century in Lvov, Austria, grew up in Poland, and in the late 1920s emigrated from the Soviet Union. Funny thing was, before she got on the boat to Brooklyn, Grandma had never left the town where she was born. It was not Grandma but the borders that kept moving! Once she got to Brooklyn, except for seasonal pilgrimages to Florida and the Catskills, she stayed put. Grandma was afraid that if she ever left the country, they'd never let her back in. She also had her suspicions about eating at the Greek diner just down the street (where she nonetheless ate every day). Though she was an immigrant, she never trusted foreigners.

The optimist proclaims that we live in the best of all possible worlds, and the pessimist fears this is true.

—James Branch Cabell (1879–1958)

We have met the enemy and he is us.

—Pogo

Often it does seem a pity that Noah and his party did not miss the boat.

—Mark Twain (1835–1910)

This world is a comedy to those who think, a tragedy to those who feel.

—Horace Walpole (1717–1797)

The age of chivalry is gone; that of sophisters, economists, and calculators has succeeded.

—Edmund Burke (1729–1797)

The fundamental cause of trouble in the world today is that the stupid are cocksure while the intelligent are full of doubt.

—Bertrand Russell (1872–1970)

*I*nsanity in individuals is something rare—but in groups, parties, nations, and epochs it is the rule.

—*Friedrich Wilhelm Nietzsche (1844–1900)*

*C*orrect me if I'm wrong, but hasn't the fine line between sanity and madness gotten finer?

—*George Price*

*M*ore than any time in history mankind faces a crossroads. One path leads to despair and utter hopelessness, the other to total extinction. Let us pray that we have the wisdom to choose correctly.

—*Woody Allen*

MISCELLANEOUS:
Work, the Economy, Money, Alcohol, etc.

Grandma was a very versatile pessimist. No matter what the subject, whether business, money, the weather—you name it—she had an appropriately gloomy sentiment at the ready. "Grandma, how's business?" I would ask. "Could be better," she'd respond. "Grandma, isn't the weather beautiful?" I would observe. "Beautiful? You call this beautiful? You could drop dead from sunstroke in such weather," she'd counter. "Grandma, do you think you'll fly to Florida this year?" I'd inquire. "Do you know what happens when a plane hits the ground at hundreds of miles an hour?"

she'd reply. If she'd lived long enough, I would have asked her, "Grandma, do you think this book will be a big hit?" Most likely, she would have answered, "Who would buy such a book?"

By the time we've made it, we've had it.

—Malcolm Forbes (1919–1990)

When things at work are busy and you're harassed and deliveries are late and people are screaming at you and you're getting cancelations, you pray for things to slow down so you can take a breath. Then when things slow down, you wonder if you'll ever do business again. Slow or busy it's never good.

—Richard Marcus

By working faithfully eight hours a day, you may eventually get to be a boss and work twelve hours a day.

—Robert Frost (1874–1963)

A conference is a gathering of important people who singly can do nothing, but together can decide that nothing can be done.

—Fred Allen (1894–1957)

*M*eetings are indispensable when you don't want to do anything.

—John Kenneth Galbraith

Their guess is as good as anybody else's.

—Will Rogers (1879–1935), on economists

In this economy, every silver lining has a dark cloud.

—Business Week *headline, March 9, 1992*

There is hardly anything in the world that some man cannot make a little worse and sell a little cheaper.

—John Ruskin (1819–1900)

I have enough money to last me the rest of my life, unless I buy something.

—Jackie Mason

*S*ave a little money each month and at the end of the year you'll be surprised at how little you have.

—Ernest Haskins

*S*ome editors are failed writers, but so are most writers.

—*T. S. Eliot (1888–1965)*

*T*he difference between journalism and literature is that journalism is unreadable and literature is not read.

—*Oscar Wilde (1854–1900)*

*W*riting is not a profession, but a vocation of unhappiness.

—*Georges Simenon (1903–1985)*

*A*dvertisements contain the only truths to be relied on in a newspaper.

—*Thomas Jefferson (1743–1826)*

*T*here are only two ways of telling the complete truth—anonymously and posthumously.

—*Thomas Sowell*

*M*en occasionally stumble over the truth, but most of them pick themselves up and hurry off as if nothing had happened.

—*Sir Winston Churchill (1874–1965)*

*A*s scarce as truth is, the supply has always been in excess of demand.

—*Josh Billings (1818–1885)*

It is by the goodness of God that in our country we have those three unspeakably precious things: freedom of speech, freedom of conscience, and the prudence never to practice either of them.

—Mark Twain (1835–1910)

*A*lcohol is the anesthesia by which we endure the operation of life.

—George Bernard Shaw (1856–1950)

I'd hate to be a teetotaller. Imagine getting up in the morning and knowing that's as good as you're going to feel all day.

—Dean Martin

*R*egarding getting sober: The good news is you get your life back. The bad news is you get your life back.

—Author unknown

*J*oin the army, see the world, meet interesting people, and kill them.

—*Author unknown*

THE OPTIMISTIC PESSIMIST

It seems a little late in the book to be confessing this, but I do have an anemic optimistic streak. You see, I have another grandmother, Grandma May. She is one of the most optimistic people I've ever known. And genetics being what they are, it's been impossible for me to banish optimistic impulses entirely. So to satisfy the sunny side of my nature, and to acknowledge Grandma May's genetic influence, I've decided to offer a few quotes here that put an optimistic spin on a pessimistic situation or outlook. Don't worry, I'm sure I'll get over it.

If . . . *you can't be a good example, then you'll just have to be a horrible warning.*

—Catherine Aird

One reassuring thing about modern art is that things can't be as bad as they are painted.

—M. Walthall Jackson

Success is the ability to go from failure to failure without losing your enthusiasm.

—Sir Winston Churchill (1874–1965)

I feel much better now that I've given up hope.

—Ashleigh Brilliant

You can always succeed at giving up.

—Bob Uyeda

"Constructive depression: How to make the best of feeling down."

—*Topic included on a videotape for stress management*

One thing about pain: It proves you're alive.

—*Ashleigh Brilliant*

Growing old is better than the alternative.

—*Variously attributed*

The longer I live the less future there is to worry about.

—*Ashleigh Brilliant*

I am guardedly optimistic about the next world, but remain cognizant of the downside risks.

—Jeremy Gluck

*D*on't take life so seriously. . . . It's not permanent.

—Kathy Holder

Razors pain you;
Rivers are damp;
Acids stain you
And drugs cause cramp;
Guns aren't lawful;
Nooses give;
Gas smells awful;
You might as well live.

—Dorothy Parker (1893–1967)

THE ULTIMATE PESSIMIST

As much as I would like to elevate Grandma Ethel to that peerless pantheon of ultimate pessimists, I can't. Not that Grandma wasn't a first-class pessimist. She was. But, as much as I love her, I have to admit that she wasn't hard core. We all knew that deep down Grandma Ethel really hoped for the best. But even though Grandma Ethel failed the ultimate pessimist test, there are still many thousands, if not millions, of people scattered across the globe who are convinced that life really is no better than the alternative. If you recognize yourself in these last few pages, count yourself among that special class of people who, like Leonore Fleischer's mother, are ultimate pessimists.

*D*o you know what a pessimist is? A man who thinks everybody as nasty as himself, and hates them for it.

—George Bernard Shaw (1856–1950)

A pessimist is one who feels bad when he feels good for fear he'll feel worse when he feels better.

—Author unknown

*W*hen two pessimists meet they shake heads instead of hands.

—Hunter Madsen

A pessimist is one who, when he has the choice of two evils, chooses both.

—*Author unknown*

A pessimist is one who has been intimately acquainted with an optimist.

—*Elbert Hubbard (1856–1915)*

*A*n optimist sees an opportunity in every calamity; a pessimist sees a calamity in every opportunity.

—Author unknown

*H*ow happy are the pessimists! What joy is theirs when they have proved there is no joy.

—Marie von Ebner-Eschenbach (1830–1916)

One has to have the courage of one's pessimism.

—Ian McEwan

When the cat's away, chances are he's been run over.

—Michael Sanders

*P*essimism in our time is infinitely more respectable than optimism: The man who foresees peace, prosperity, and a decline in juvenile delinquency is a negligent and vacuous fellow. The man who foresees catastrophe has a gift of insight which insures that he will become a radio commentator, an editor of Time, or go to Congress.

—John Kenneth Galbraith

*M*y pessimism goes to the point of suspecting the sincerity of pessimists.

—Jean Rostand (1894–1977)

I was going to buy a copy of The Power of Positive Thinking, *and then I thought: What the hell good would that do?*

—*Ronnie Shakes*